mission on a mountain

Cecil P. Golann

222

Cecil P. Golann

Mission on a mountain

The Story of Abraham and Isaac

illustrated by H. Hechtkopf

Lerner Publications Company
Minneapolis, Minnesota

AN
OUTSTANDING
SELECTION
FROM
Israel

First published in the United States of America 1975
by Lerner Publications Company, Minneapolis, Minnesota.

Copyright © 1974 by Massada Press Ltd., Jerusalem, Israel.

International Standard Book Number: 0–8225–0363–8
Library of Congress Catalog Card Number: 73–7498.

Printed in Israel and Bound in U.S.A.

ong, long ago, an old man with a thick white beard came to Palestine, the Holy Land of the Bible. The man's name was Abraham, which means "father of many." Abraham was a generous man, and he opened his heart to all. Whenever strangers passed by his tent, Abraham gave them food and drink. He also gave them fine clothes, and even silver and gold. But most important, Abraham taught men to have faith in the one true God.

Abraham's guests always thanked him for sharing his blessings with them. But Abraham replied, "Don't thank me, thank God. God created all things, and He cares for us all. He gives us bread for our hunger and water for our thirst. Bless God, and be blessed by Him."

Long before coming to Palestine, Abraham had married a beautiful woman named Sarah. Abraham and Sarah were very happy at first, and they looked forward to having many children. The years passed quickly, but no children were born to them. For a long time, Abraham and Sarah prayed to God for a son. Still, Sarah bore no children. Abraham and Sarah grew very old, and sorrow filled their hearts.

When Abraham was 99 years old, he and Sarah journeyed into the land of the Philistine people, near the Mediterranean Sea. Abimelech was the king of the Philistines, and he respected Abraham for his great age and wisdom. Soon the king and Abraham became good friends.

One day Abraham found Abimelech in tears. When Abraham asked the king why he was weeping, the king said, "I have been married many years, but still I have no son. When I die, there will be no one to take my place on the throne. This saddens me, and it makes my people restless."

Abraham was moved by the king's words, for he too had no son. He pitied Abimelech and prayed to God to send the king a son. God answered Abraham's prayer, and a son was born to Abimelech and his wife. "Praise be to the Lord," said Abraham, "for His mercy is great."

Abraham's unselfish deed did not go unnoticed. The angels in heaven were touched by it, and they pleaded with God to send Abraham a son too. God listened to His angels and granted their request. At last, a son was born to Abraham and Sarah. Because the child brought great joy, he was named "Isaac," which means "laughter." Isaac was a blessed infant, and many people came to see and admire him.

No child was ever as precious to his parents as Isaac was to Abraham and Sarah. Abraham now had all that a man could ask for. He was blessed by the Lord in every way, and his goodness was known to all.

As the years passed, Isaac became a strong, handsome boy. One year, Abraham decided to give a magnificent party to celebrate Isaac's birthday. Now it was the custom in those times for a wealthy and important man like Abraham to share his good fortune with the poor whenever he gave a feast. But Abraham was forgetful this time, and he did not invite even one poor man to his party.

Perhaps no one would have said anything about Abraham's sin. After all, even the best of men can fall into the ways of error. But there is one enemy of both God and man who is always watching for human sin—*Satan!* He especially wanted to disgrace Abraham in the eyes of God. So when Abraham forgot to invite any poor people to his party, Satan decided to set a trap for him.

Before long, Isaac's birthday arrived. The party Abraham gave for Isaac was splendid beyond belief. Abraham's great tent was decorated with branches of balsam, laurel, and fragrant myrtle. Sweet scents and joyous music filled the air. Long tables were placed in the tent and covered with great quantities of food and drink. There were breads and wines, and the meat of lambs and goats. There were pomegranates and figs, apricots and grapes. There were almonds and honey, oil and olives. And everything was served in beautiful vessels.

Dressed in their finest garments, the guests began to arrive. Some came by foot, some came by donkey, and others came by camel. One by one, they congratulated Isaac on his birthday. Isaac stood tall and proud, and he welcomed his guests graciously.

Once the party began, Abraham was kept busy entertaining all the guests. They were important people, and Abraham wanted them to have a good time. Sarah also bustled about the tent. She made sure that everyone had enough to eat and drink.

Just when everyone was having a good time, Satan came to the party. But instead of coming as himself, he came disguised as a beggar. Dressed in rags, Satan begged Abraham and Sarah for some food. But they had no time for the "beggar," and they turned him away empty-handed. Satan's trap had worked! By refusing to share their good fortune, Abraham and Sarah had sinned.

As Satan crept away from Abraham's tent, he said, "Woe, woe to you, Abraham! You had no time for the beggar. You were too busy with your guests. Alas, alas, Sarah. It was the same with you."

Satan now believed that he could bring shame and dishonor upon Abraham. Boldly, he went before God and accused Abraham of sinning. "Behold how wicked Abraham has become," cried Satan. "You answered his prayers. You gave him a son. Now he has forgotten You. Now he disobeys You by turning away the poor."

"I have faith in Abraham," God replied. "It was wrong of him to turn away a beggar, but he is still a kind and holy man. He has not forgotten Me."

"When did he last offer sheep or goats to You?" Satan asked. (Satan knew that Abraham had been neglectful.)

"Never mind about sheep and goats!" God angrily replied. "If I asked him to, Abraham would sacrifice even his beloved *son!*"

"Put Abraham to the test then," mocked Satan. "Ask him to sacrifice Isaac. See if he obeys You."

"So be it," said God. "Then you shall see whether Abraham loves and obeys Me."

Early the next morning, God said to Abraham, "Take now your son, whom you love, and sacrifice him as a sign of your obedience to Me."

Abraham was stunned into silence. Had this greatest of sacrifices *really* been asked of him? He prayed that it had not.

God repeated the command. Abraham was to take Isaac into the land of Moriah. God would give him a sign when he reached the place for the sacrifice.

Finally, Abraham gathered the strength to speak. "Should not a priest perform such a sacrifice?" he asked. Then, in a soft, pleading voice, he whispered, "Lord, I am not a priest."

God sternly replied, "When the time comes for you to sacrifice Isaac, I will consecrate you as a priest."

Abraham was deeply saddened by the mission God had given him, but he accepted it. Putting his trust in the Lord, he went off to fetch Isaac.

As Abraham walked toward his tent, his eyes filled with tears. "How shall I part Isaac from his mother?" he thought. "Sarah loves the boy as much as I do, and she will never let me take him from her."

Abraham could not bring himself to tell Sarah the truth. So instead, he told her that he was taking Isaac to a place where the boy could learn more about serving the Lord. At first, Sarah wept at the thought of being separated from Isaac. But in the end, she agreed to let him go. "My days will be empty without Isaac," she said. "But I want him to be wise in the ways of God."

Sarah dressed Isaac in a finely woven robe and gave him plenty of food for the journey. "Take good care of him," she begged Abraham. Then she waved good-bye as Abraham and Isaac set forth on their journey. Soon they went out of sight. Weeping, Sarah returned to her tent. "Who knows when I shall see them again," she sobbed.

As Abraham led Isaac through the wilderness, Satan watched them from afar. He could see that Abraham was obeying God's command, and this made him very angry. "Abraham *must* sin," thought Satan. "I will tempt him to disobey the Lord."

Satan disguised himself as an old man so that Abraham would not recognize him. Then he approached Abraham, saying, "Are you really going to sacrifice your only son? Isaac is good. He has done no wrong. Why then will you do away with him? Surely this cannot be God's will. God would never tell a man to sacrifice his only son."

But Abraham was wise. He recognized Satan at once, and he ignored him. "Only Satan would say such words to me," thought Abraham. "Only Satan would tempt me to disobey the Lord's command."

Despite all of Satan's tricks, Abraham remained firm in his purpose. Seeing this, Satan went away.

A while later, Satan decided to tempt Isaac. This time, he came in the form of a handsome young man. "Don't you know that your father is going to kill you?" he asked Isaac. "Why do you go along with him? Return to your mother and save yourself from destruction."

But Abraham again recognized Satan, and he warned Isaac.
"Pay no attention to this person!" Abraham shouted. "He
is Satan in disguise, and he is trying to make us disobey God."

Even as Satan left, he planned yet another trap for Abraham
and Isaac. "*This* time I shall not fail," he vowed.

Before long, Abraham and Isaac came to a brook. They tried to cross it, but as they went on, the brook became deeper and deeper. Isaac was soon up to his neck in water, and he feared for his life.

"Do not be afraid," said Abraham. "This is just another one of Satan's tricks. He is trying to prevent us from carrying out the work of God."

Then, with rage in his voice, Abraham lashed out at Satan: "How dare you block our path like this! Away with you, Satan!"

Frightened by Abraham's anger, Satan went away. The brook also disappeared with him. Thus Satan had failed *again* to lead Abraham astray from God's command.

Free of Satan, Abraham and Isaac continued on toward the place of sacrifice. The sun beat down on them from a cloudless sky. From time to time, they saw a bird flying overhead or a snake slithering through the bushes. Then, on the third day of their journey, Abraham and Isaac saw a mountain in the distance. On the mountain was a pillar of fire that reached all the way to the sky, and on top of the pillar was a thick, swirling cloud.

Abraham took this as the sign God had promised him. The Lord would receive Isaac here — on Mount Moriah. Turning to Isaac, Abraham said, "God has sent us to offer a sacrifice on the mountain ahead. We must hurry."

"But, father, we have no sheep or goats," said Isaac. "How then can we offer a sacrifice?"

The moment had come for Abraham to tell Isaac the truth. "Isaac, my son, I must kill you."

Isaac froze where he was standing. *"Kill me?"* he gasped. "Father, what wrong have I done? If I have been wicked, punish me. But do not slay me with that sharp knife in your hand."

Abraham wept. "Alas, my child, I have no choice."

Isaac could not understand. "If only my mother were here," he cried. "She would beg you on her knees to spare me. But since she is not here, I myself must pray you not to kill me."

"God has commanded me to sacrifice you," Abraham tried to explain. "I must obey God and carry out this mission."

"Do the Lord's bidding then," Isaac said meekly. "But spare my mother. Let her think that I am still alive, and that I have gone somewhere else to live."

"You are goodness itself," murmured Abraham. He wrung his hands in sorrow as he thought of slaying his blessed child. "Isaac, do you accept your fate?" he asked.

"Yes," said Isaac. "I will do as the Lord commands."

Abraham and Isaac were united in their desire to do God's will. Together, they climbed Mount Moriah and came to the place for the sacrifice. There, they built an altar.

After wood had been placed on the altar, Abraham slowly began to bind Isaac for the sacrifice. "Hurry, father, hurry!" cried out Isaac. "Bind my hands and feet tightly so that I may not struggle when you take the knife to kill me."

Abraham wept openly as he bound Isaac upon the altar.
"Isaac," he cried, "when you die, I shall die too."

The wind rustled the branches of a nearby tree, and a bird began to sing sadly. To Abraham's ears, the bird seemed to be saying:

"Poor father, grieving mother,
Who will carry on your line?
Who will comfort you in your old age?
What meaning has life now?
Oh God! Oh angels of God!
Must this blessed boy be sacrificed?
Must a father kill his only son?"

As Abraham looked down upon Isaac, he cried out, "Dear God, give me the strength to carry out this mission!"

God watched all this from heaven, and He saw that Abraham was ready to carry out His command. God also saw that Abraham was weeping over his beloved son Isaac. Seeing this, God called His angels before Him and said, "Behold Abraham's devotion to Me. Can anyone doubt his faith now?"

The angels pitied Abraham, and they wept for him. Suddenly, God said to one of His angels, "Go at once and save Isaac from the sacrifice!" The angel bowed his head and left to do the Lord's bidding.

Just as Abraham was about to slay Isaac, the angel appeared. "Abraham!" he called out. "Stop at once! Do not raise your hand against the boy."

"Whom shall I obey? God or you?" asked Abraham.

Then, in all His majesty and power, God said to Abraham, "You were willing to give Me your son, your only son. This is proof enough that you love Me."

Rejoicing, Abraham untied Isaac and raised him from the altar. Together, they thanked God for His mercy. Then Abraham asked, "Did You know that I would sacrifice Isaac to You?"

"Yes," God answered.

"Why then did you put me through this test?" asked Abraham.

"Because I wished the world to learn about you," God replied. "Now the world will know why I have chosen you above all other men."

Abraham turned around and saw a ram caught in a bush by its horns. He took the ram and sacrificed it instead of Isaac. And God was pleased with the sacrifice.

By demonstrating his faith and obedience, Abraham had set an example for all people to follow. God told Abraham that a temple would be built on Mount Moriah to stand as a reminder of Abraham's devotion to Him. It would be raised on the very spot where Abraham had built the altar.

God also told Abraham his descendants would remember that a ram had been sacrificed instead of Isaac. Hebrew people would always celebrate the coming of each new year by blowing a ram's horn. This would remind them of Abraham's and Isaac's devotion to God.

Then God said to Abraham, "Because you have obeyed Me, I will bless you and make your name great. Your descendants will be as numerous as the stars in the heavens, and as the grains of sand on the seashore. And in your seed shall all the nations of the earth be blessed."

After hearing these words, Abraham and Isaac returned home with the favor of the Lord upon them.

GODDARD UNITED METHODIST CHURCH
Box 331
Goddard, Ks. 67052

GODDARD UNITED METHODIST CHURCH
Box 331
Goddard, Ks. 67052